UNTOLD PRICE ACTION TRADING SECRETS

Master Pivot Points, Market Direction, and Trend Integration for Consistent Profits in Forex & Beyond (a quick read)

by
Nana Osae

DISCLAIMER

This book is for educational and informational purposes only. The author and publisher make no representations or warranties with respect to the accuracy, applicability, fitness, or completeness of the contents of this book. The information contained in this book is subject to change without notice.

Trademarks mentioned in this material belong to their respective owners and are used for informational purposes only. The author and publisher are not associated with any product or vendor mentioned in this book.

TABLE OF CONTENTS

DISCLAIMER

CHAPTER ONE

INTRODUCTION

CHAPTER TWO

UNCOVERING VALID PIVOT POINTS

Defining price swings

Pivot points

Valid pivot point

CHAPTER THREE

DETERMINING MARKET DIRECTION

Key notes to keep in mind

CHAPTER FOUR

COMBINING MICRO AND MACRO TRENDS IN TRADING?

CHAPTER FIVE

THE NAKED EXIT METHOD

CHAPTER SIX

AN IMPORTANT TRADING SECRET

CHAPTER SEVEN

RISK MANAGEMENT & TRADING PSYCHOLOGY

CHAPTER EIGHT

FINAL THOUGHTS & FAQS

CHAPTER ONE

INTRODUCTION

W hen I began my journey into learning the intricacies of trading in the forex market, I encountered a significant hurdle: comprehending market structure. Seasoned traders seemed to effortlessly identify patterns such as higher highs, lower highs, higher lows, and lower lows on the charts. However, for me, deciphering the specific price points that truly constituted valid pivot points—those indicative of a genuine higher high or lower high, and a higher low or lower low—proved to be a challenging puzzle to solve. Watch the video titled, "The hurdle", listed here, to understand what my problem was better.

In my pursuit of comprehension, I sought guidance from various trading experts, eager to unravel the complexities of market structure. Regrettably, their explanations often left me more bewildered than enlightened. Some touted the Zigzag indicator, others leaned on the Parabolic SAR, and a few underscored the significance of market rhythm. However, none of these approaches furnished the objective methodology I sought—a clear-cut method to decipher market structure and engage in profitable trading without resorting to guesswork.

Determined to find a solution, I persisted for several years until I uncovered a powerful naked approach that has since transformed my trading endeavours. My unwavering dedication and persistence have finally paid off, marking a pivotal moment in my trading journey.

In this easy-to-follow guide, I am excited to present a straightforward yet robust method for precisely grasping market structure and determining market direction. I have compiled this material to address common questions that traders need to answer in order to trade effectively:

- What truly validates a pivot point?
- How can you accurately determine the current market direction?
- What indicators suggest a potential shift in market direction?
- How do you distinguish between a macro trend and a micro trend?
- How do you effectively combine macro and micro trends in your trading strategy?
- What practical approach can you use to exit a trade without resorting to guesswork?; and last but not least,
- What valuable trading secrets merit careful consideration?

Join me as I demystify these crucial issues, providing you with a practical toolkit to enhance your trading success.

To facilitate understanding, this manual is complemented by a series of videos, listed here, that expound on the knowledge shared in these pages. The synergy of written and visual content provides a comprehensive learning experience. While this manual intentionally remains concise, featuring only a select number of exercises, the additional videos, listed here, complete with a series of exercises, enrich the overall educational package. I am optimistic that the insights presented guide, coupled with the accompanying videos, will have a lasting and transformative impact on your trading education.

It is worth highlighting that, as a comprehensive resource on price action trading, while the term 'forex pairs' is consistently employed throughout the material, the lessons presented transcend the forex market. The principles shared can be seamlessly applied to a diverse array of financial assets, including stocks, bonds, commodities, currencies, and derivatives. This adaptability broadens the scope of applicability, catering to a wide spectrum of traders across different markets.

Without hesitation, let us delve into the crux of the matter. Join me on this transformative journey as we unlock the secrets of naked trading and market structure, and confidently determine market direction. Together, we will navigate the intricacies of trading with clarity and precision.

CHAPTER TWO

UNCOVERING VALID PIVOT POINTS

A pivot point marks an important juncture in the market where price reaches a turning point and initiates a reversal. However, not all pivot points or reversal points are worth-considering. Some are valid and some are invalid. To discern what qualifies as a valid pivot point, it is imperative to first understand the concept of price swing.

Defining Price Swings

A price swing is characterized by a sequence of candles moving in a specific direction. In simpler terms, when the market trends in a particular direction with a series of candles, it forms a price swing. For a visual representation, please refer to the illustration in Figure 1.

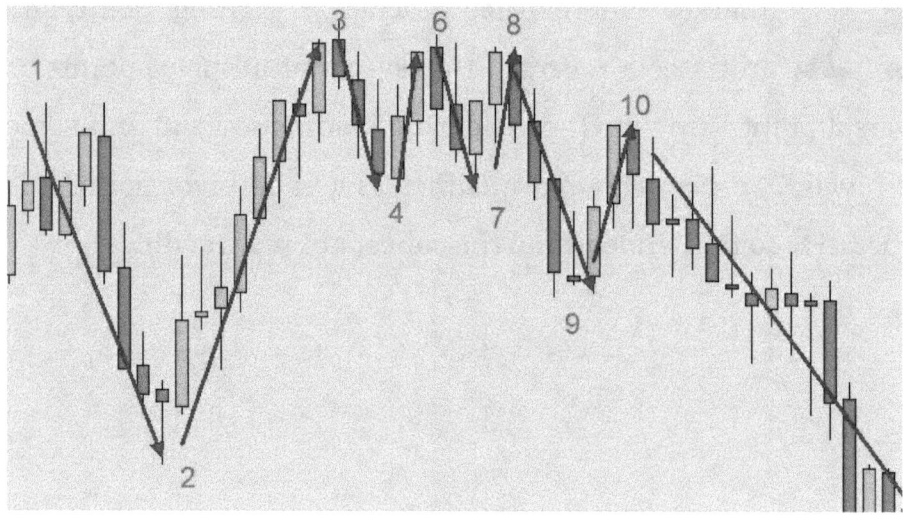

Figure 1: Each arrow marks a price swing

As illustrated in Figure 1, each arrow serves as a marker for a price swing on the price chart. For example, the transition from price point 1 to point 2 signifies a distinct price swing, mirroring the movement from point 2 to point 3, indicating another swing, and so forth. Likewise, the shift from point 3 to point 4 represents yet another swing in the dynamic forex market. These arrows visually show the sequential swings that unfold within the market trends.

Distinguishing Valid And Invalid Swings

In the markets, there are two distinct types of swings – valid and invalid. A valid swing is characterized by the presence of at least three candles, with a noticeable space between at least two candles within the swing. Conversely, an invalid swing is defined by either having fewer than three candles within it or lacking a gap between the high and low of any two candles within that swing.

In essence, a valid swing necessitates a minimum of three candles and a gap between the high and low of any two candles within it. Any swing lacking these attributes is deemed an invalid swing.

Exercise 1

Refer to Figure 1 and answer the following questions:
- Is Swing 1-2 valid or invalid?
- Is Swing 2-3 valid or invalid?
- Is Swing 3-4 valid or invalid?
- Is Swing 4-5 valid or invalid?
- Is Swing 5-6 valid or invalid?
- Is Swing 6-7 valid or invalid?
- Is Swing 7-8 valid or invalid?
- Is Swing 8-9 valid or invalid?
- Is Swing 9-10 valid or invalid?

Please complete the above exercise before reading the next section.

Based on the explanation given for qualifying swings, Swing 1-2 is valid; swing is 2-3 valid; swing 3-4 is invalid; Swing 4-5 is invalid; Swing 5-6 is invalid; Swing 6-7 is invalid; Swing 7-8 is invalid; Swing 8-9 is valid; and swing 9-10 is valid.

Expand your understanding of swings by watching the video titled *"Distinguishing valid and invalid swings"* listed here.

Now that you have gained an understanding of what a price swing is and the distinction between valid and invalid swings, let us shift our focus to pivot points.

Pivot Points

As previously mentioned, pivot points, commonly known simply as pivots, denote turning points in the market where a reversal occurs. In Figure 1, the reversal points marked as 1, 2, 3, 4, 5, 7, 8, 9, and 10 are identified as pivot points.

However, as previously mentioned, it is crucial to note that not all pivot points meet the criteria for validity in this trading model. This distinction is of utmost importance. Possessing a trading model or a set of objective rules to validate market behaviour is essential for analysing the market without relying on guesswork.

Thus, for a turning point to be considered as valid, it must meet specific criteria. In the pursuit of objectively reading market structure and trading without relying on guesswork, the identification of valid pivot points is paramount. So, what constitutes valid pivot points, and how do we identify them? The next section delves into precisely that.

Valid Pivot Point

A valid pivot point marks a clear moment where the price undergoes a reversal, initiating a valid swing in the opposite direction. To consider a pivot point valid, it requires the presence of a valid price swing preceding it and another valid price swing following it. This criterion serves as a clear indicator of a definitive shift in market direction.

Therefore, for a pivot point to attain validity, it must satisfy two essential conditions:

1. It must be preceded by a valid swing.

2. It must be followed by a valid swing.To visualize this concept, kindly refer to Figure 2 below:

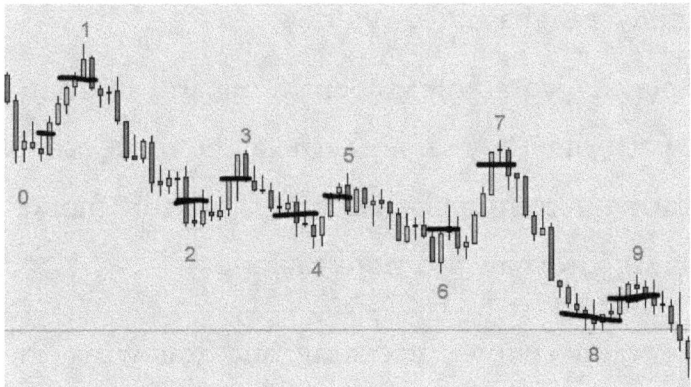

Figure 2: Space between two candles in a swing

In Figure 2, the apparent gap between the high of Candle 0 and the low of Candle 1 validates Swing 0-1. Furthermore, the space between the low of Candle 1 and the high of Candle 2 establishes Swing 1-2 as a valid swing. Therefore, it can be asserted that Pivot Point 1, being preceded and followed by valid price swings (Swing 0-1 and Swing 1-2), is valid.

In essence, Pivot 1 is also both preceded and followed by valid swings, establishing its validity.

For a comprehensive understanding, I recommend watching my video titled *"Valid pivot points"* listed here.

Valid pivot points represent regions where the price has undergone a significant shift. It is crucial to emphasize that valid pivot points are precisely the points we refer to as higher highs and higher lows or lower highs and lower lows.

Valid pivot points play a pivotal role in identifying and analysing market trends and patterns. They serve as crucial reference points for traders, facilitating a comprehensive assessment of market structure and enabling informed decisions making.

By identifying the valid swings preceding and following the pivot points, traders can pinpoint potential areas of support and resistance. This insight provides a valuable understanding of the market's directional bias, aiding in more informed trading decisions.

It is essential to highlight that, in technical analysis, traders often combine pivot points with other custom indicators and tools like trend lines, moving averages, and oscillators to confirm trends and build robust trading strategies. However, the focus of this guide is to empower traders to engage in profitable trading without relying on additional indicators – hence the title, Naked Forex Trading Secrets.

Now let us try hands on some exercises.

Exercise 2

In Figure 3, indicate whether the labelled pivot points are valid or invalid.

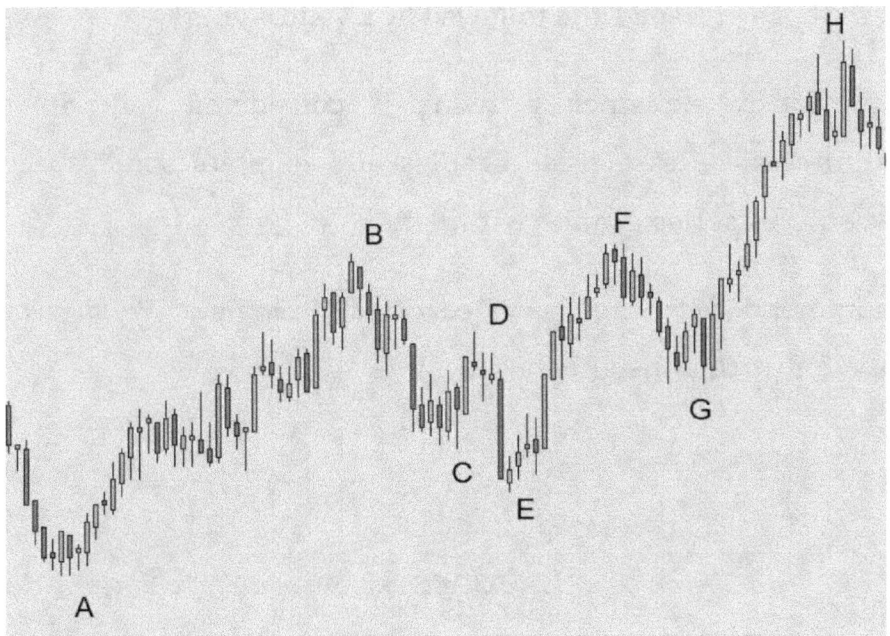

Figure 3: Valid or invalid pivot point?

A = Valid or invalid?

B = Valid or invalid?

C = Valid or invalid?

D = Valid or invalid?

E = Valid or invalid?

H = Valid or invalid?

Complete the above exercise before reading the next section.

Answer

All the pivot points are valid. Each pivot point satisfies the criteria of being both preceded and followed by a valid swing.

As previously explained a swing is considered valid if it encompasses at least three candles and exhibits some space between at least two candles within it.

I recommend watching the video titled *"Exercise 2: Valid pivot points"* for further insights.

Exercise 3

Identify the invalid pivots in Figure 4.

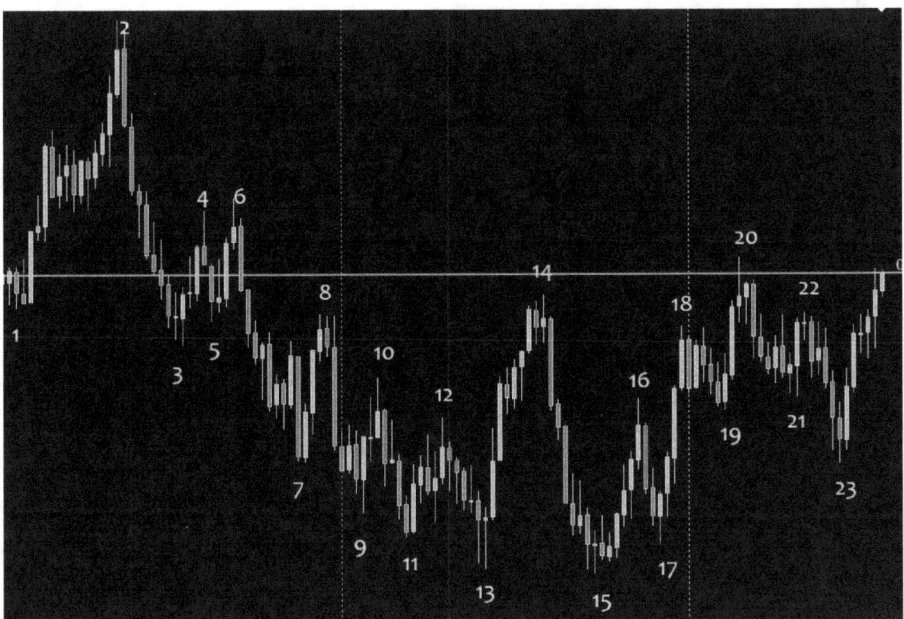

Figure 4: Identify price swings as valid or invalid

Complete the above exercise before reading the next section.

Answer

The invalid pivots in Exercise 3 include points 4, 5, 9, 10, 18, and 19. This classification arises from the fact that these points were either not preceded or followed by a valid price swing. To illustrate, pivot point 5 is deemed invalid as it lacked a preceding valid swing. Similarly, pivot point 4, not having a valid swing following it, is considered an invalid high.

Mastering the identification of valid pivot points establishes a robust foundation for understanding market structure and making well-informed trading decisions. The skill of recognizing these pivotal turning points contributes to a more objective analysis, empowering you to navigate the market with confidence and seize profitable opportunities.

The concept of valid pivot points clarifies the rationale behind selectively considering certain points and skipping others. In essence, when analysing or reading market structure, it is the valid pivot points that are considered, while the invalid ones are disregarded.

Having explored the significance of valid pivot points, let us progress to the next section, where we delve into determining the current trend direction of the market. Starting from Chapter 3, unless explicitly stated otherwise, terms such as 'higher high,' 'higher low,' 'lower high,' 'lower low,' 'high,' 'low,' 'pivot point,' or 'pivot' will consistently signify the same concept – a valid pivot point.

Exercise 4

Which of the pivot points labelled in Figure 5 are valid?

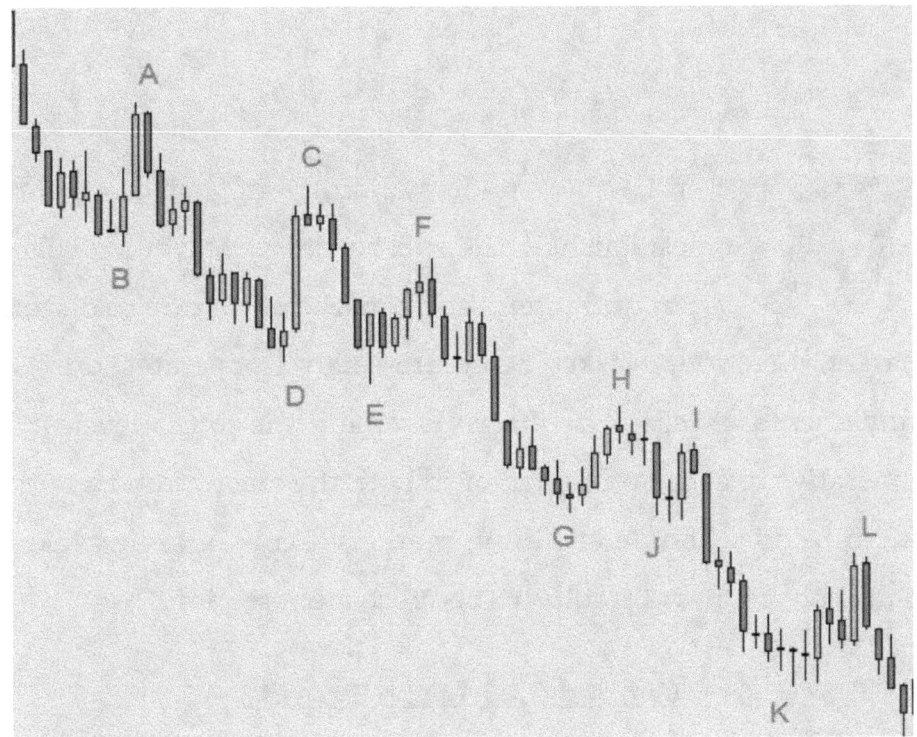

Figure 5: Valid and invalid pivot points

The ample explanations already provided should suffice in helping you to answer the question effortlessly. However, if needed, you may watch this video titled *"Figure 5: valid and invalid pivot points"* listed here, for the answers.

CHAPTER THREE

DETERMINING MARKET DIRECTION

With the understanding of pivot points established, the subsequent endeavour revolves around interpreting market structure to discern market direction. Market structure analysis operates on two fundamental levels – the macro level and the micro level. It is imperative to consistently factor in both the macro trend and the micro trend when determining market direction. Let us take a look at both types of trends in the subsequent sections.

What Is A Macro Trend?

The macro-trend signifies the overarching market direction at the pivot point level, often referred to as the bigger market direction. This determination is made by analysing the market's trajectory through the framework of pivot points. Hence, when utilizing pivot points for assessing market direction, one essentially embraces a macro perspective, delving into the bigger picture in chart analysis. It is crucial to mention that this approach is applicable to any chart or timeframe.

Determining The Macro Trend Direction Of The Market.

Macro trends serve as crucial indicators, providing traders with indispensable insights into the overarching trajectory of the market. Seasoned traders adeptly scrutinize macro trends by discerning the presence of higher highs and higher lows, identifying lower highs and lower lows, or analysing highs and lows within the market. The determination of these trends is optimally achieved through a comprehensive analysis of pivot points formed by price swings.

Low pivots typically exhibit a V-shaped pattern, while high pivots showcase a Λ-shaped pattern. If a high pivot is higher than the preceding high pivot, it is termed a higher high, and if a high pivot is lower than the previous high pivot it is referred to as a lower high. If a low pivot is higher than the previous one, it is termed a higher low, whereas a lower low occurs when a low pivot is lower than the preceding low pivot. See Figure 6.

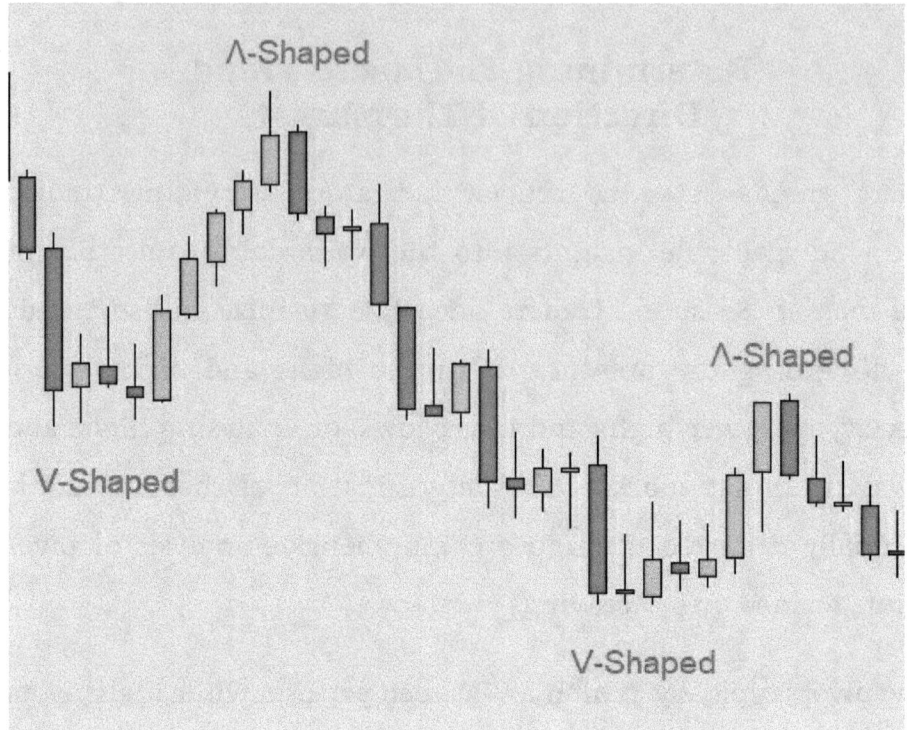

Figure 6: Lows are V-shaped and highs are Λ-shaped

Bullish Macro Trend

A bullish macro trend is established when higher high and higher low pivot points are observed. This is visually depicted in Figure 7.

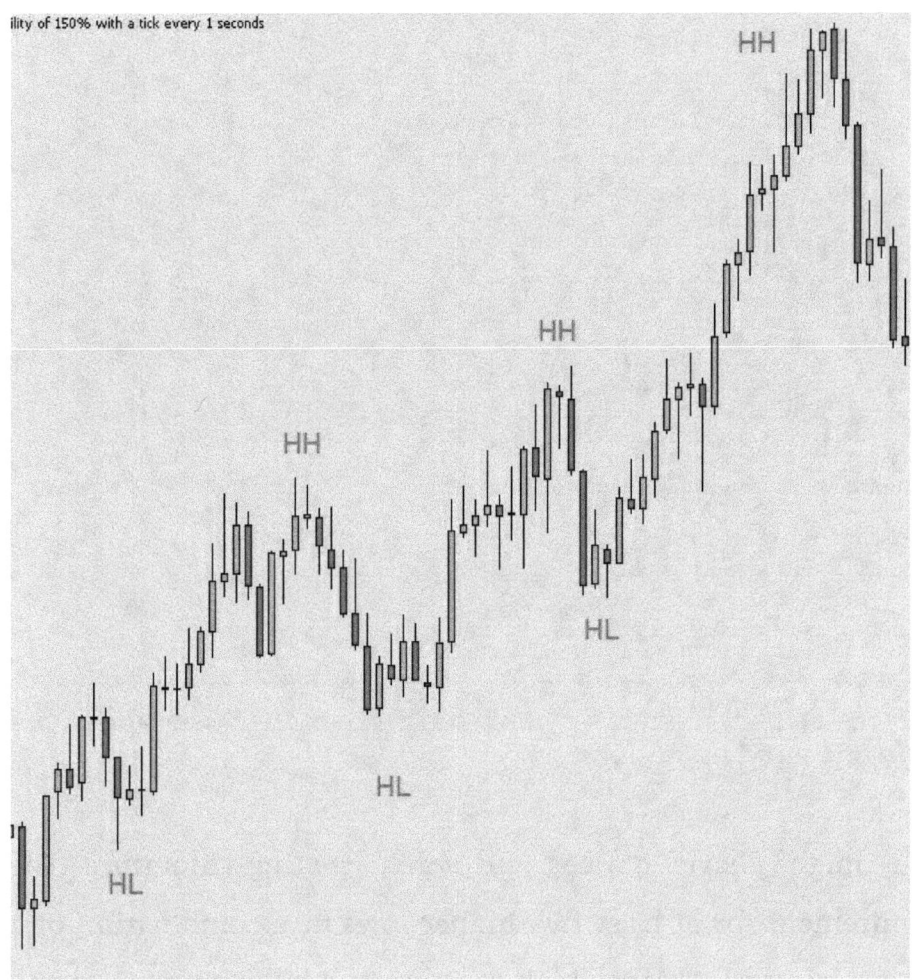

Figure 7: Bullish Macro Trend

When To Confirm A Bullish Macro Trend Change

If a candle closes above the high of the last high, the macro trend is considered bullish. Refer to Figure 8 for a visual representation.

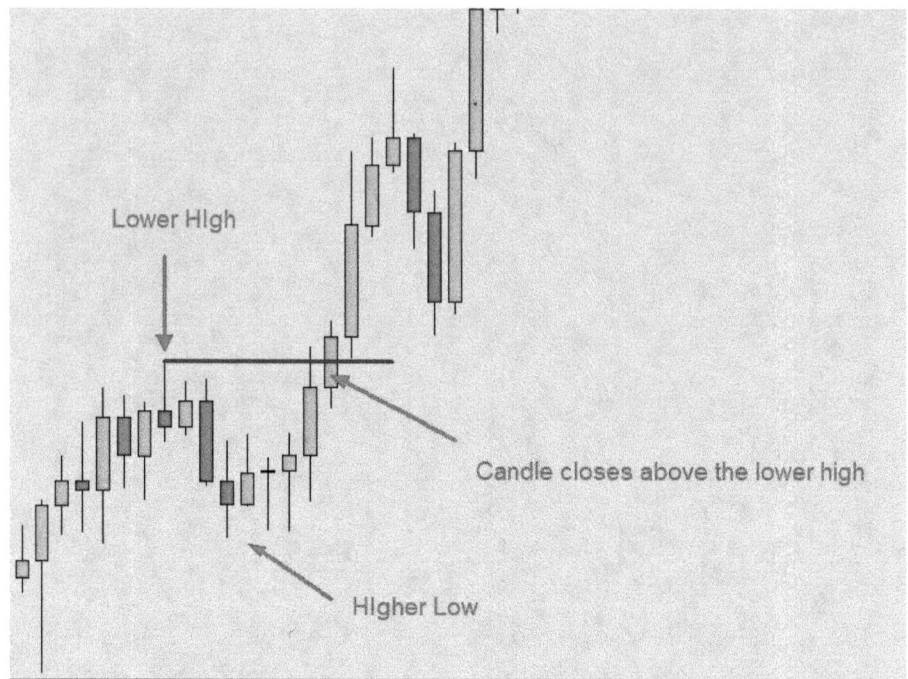

Figure 8: Uptrend starts when a bullish candle closes above the high of a valid pivot point.

You might have noticed in some trading literature the requirement for at least two higher lows or a combination of a higher low and a higher high to confirm a bullish price change. While this approach is not incorrect, trading fundamentally revolves around adhering to a defined set of rules. The key is to stay disciplined and consistent with your established rules.

If the market consistently forms higher lows and higher highs with its pivot points, it signals an bullish trend at the macro level.

Bearish Macro Trend

A bearish macro trend is established when lower highs and lower low pivot points are observed. This is depicted in Figure 9.

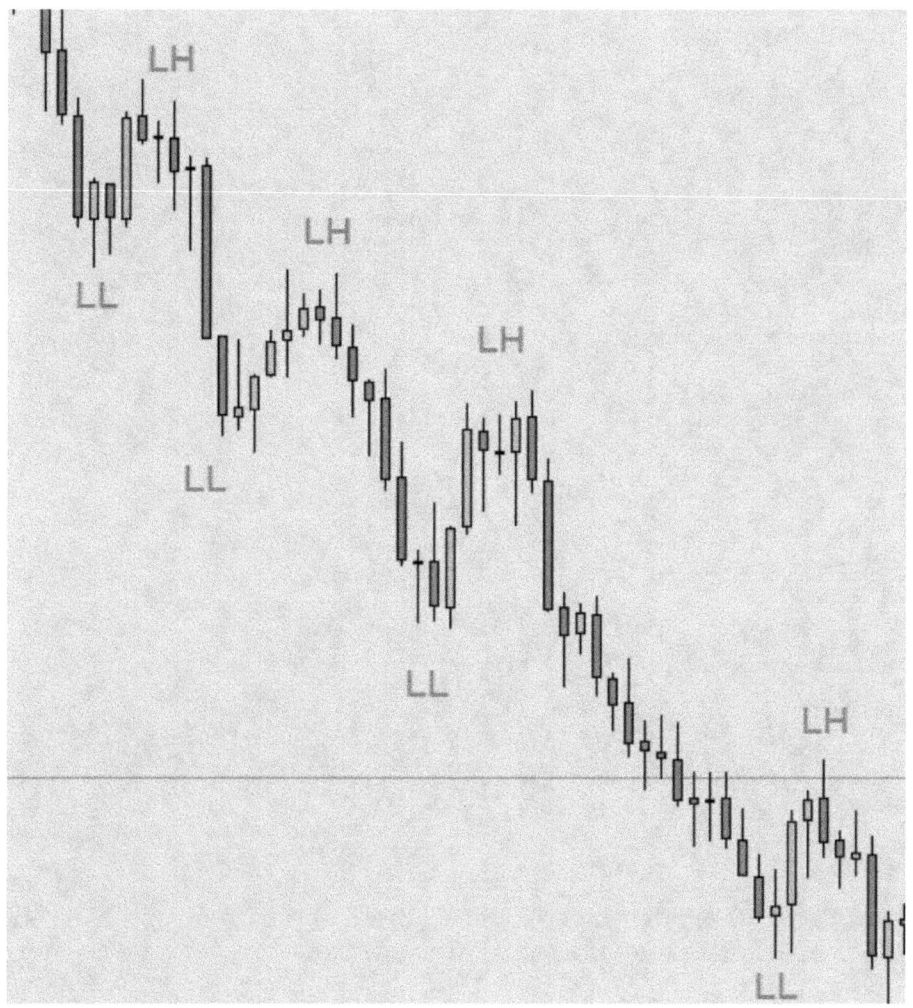

Figure 9: Bearish macro trend

When To Confirm A Bearish Macro Trend Change

If a candle closes below the low of the last low, whether it is a lower low or just a low pivot point, the macro trend is considered to have shifted to the downside. Refer to Figure 10 for visual representation.

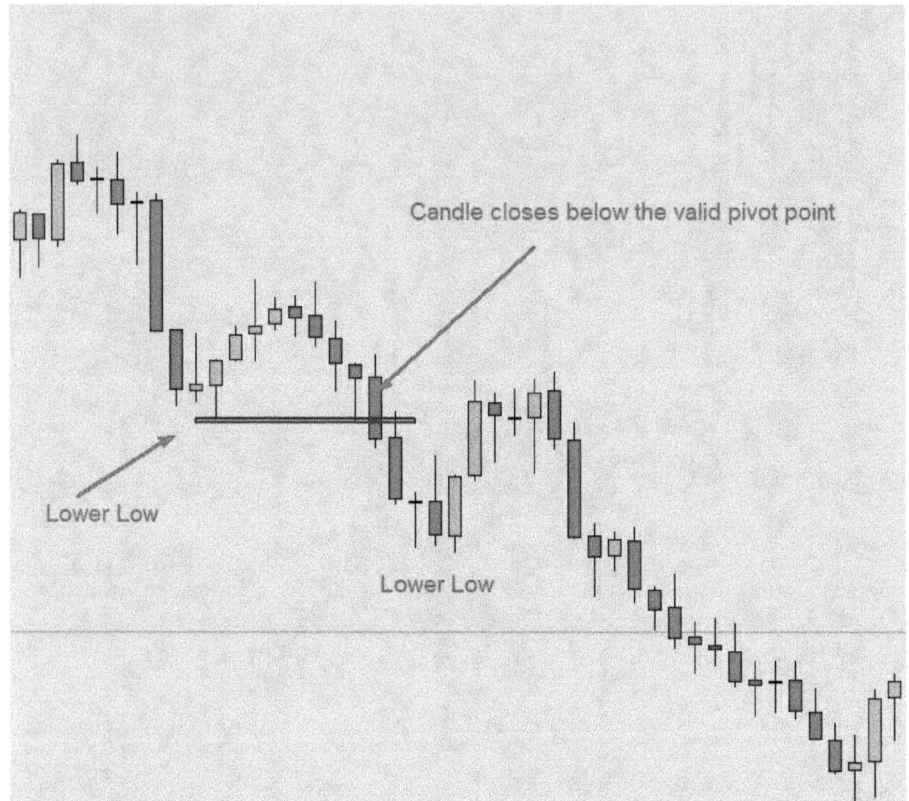

Figure 10: Bearish macro trend starts when a bearish candle closes below the low of a valid pivot point.

Again, in the trading literature, you may have come across the idea that confirming a bearish price change necessitates at least two lower lows or a combination of a lower low and a lower high. While this perspective is valid, the crux of successful trading lies in adhering to a well-defined set of rules that you establish for yourself. Consistency in following these rules is paramount.

To truly grasp market trends, consider this: if the market keeps forming lower lows and lower highs, it is on a downward trend. Traders zero in on pivot points from price swings to spot these bigger trends. These pivotal moments mark significant price changes, serving as crucial markers to understand the larger trend. Analysing these pivot points gives insights into the overall market direction, helping traders make smarter decisions.

For an even clearer understanding, check out this video titled *"Confirming a bearish macro trend change"* listed here.

Also watch the video titled *"A breakdown of macro trends"* listed here. It provides a thorough breakdown of macro trends, offering valuable insights into macro trends and how to interpret them. Stressing the significance of pivot points in gauging market directions, the video extends further guidance on integrating macro trend analysis into your trading strategies.

Understanding macro trends and recognizing their pivotal role in market analysis is fundamental for trading success. By acknowledging both macro and micro trends, traders can cultivate a comprehensive view of the market, facilitating well-informed decision-making. It is crucial not to underestimate the micro trend, as exclusive focus on the macro trend may lead to frequent hits to stop losses. Hence, maintaining a balanced understanding of both trend levels is imperative for effective trading.

What Is A Micro Trend?

A micro trend signifies the market direction within a price swing. The idea of a price swing has been thoroughly explored in Chapter Two. If necessary, feel free to re-visit that section to refresh your understanding of price swings.

Determining The Micro Trend Direction Of The Market

Unlike macro trends, which are established by pivot points, micro trends take shape within price swings. A micro trend becomes apparent when there is an engulfing pattern within a price swing, serving as the transition point from one swing to another. For a demonstration of this concept, refer to the video titled *"Determining the micro trend direction of the market"*.

An engulfing pattern manifests when the market displays a prevalence of either bullish or bearish candlestick formations. Should the candlesticks reflect a prevalence of bullish activity, it signals an upward micro trend. Conversely, if the candlesticks depict a prevalence of bearish activity, it indicates a downward micro trend. Refer to Figure 11 for visual illustration.

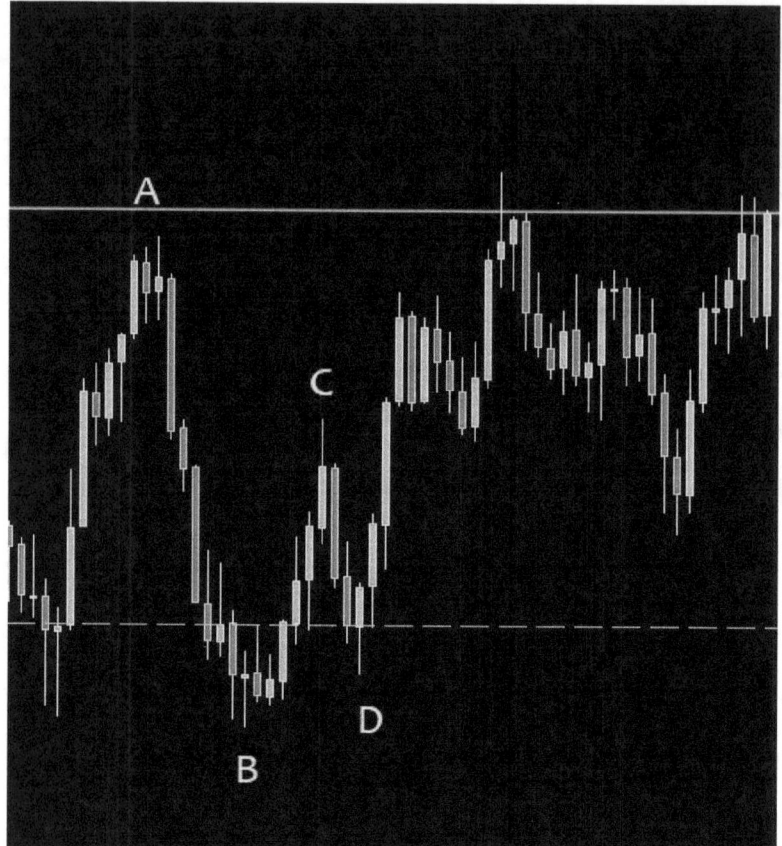

Figure 11: Micro tends and macro trends

Referring to Figure 11, the swing from point A to point B distinctly showcases the dominance of bears. However, the presence of a second bullish candlestick after point B signifies the establishment of an upward bullish micro trend.

As observed, the formation of the upward micro-trend marks the conclusion of the swing from Point A to B and kick-starts the swing from B to C.

In applying this insight to your trading, it is crucial to note that for a bullish micro trend to be confirmed, the bullish candles should close above the preceding significant bearish candle with its body. Conversely, for a bearish micro trend confirmation, the bears should close below the preceding significant bullish candle with its body.

Bullish Micro Trend

As mentioned earlier, a bullish micro trend emerges in a bullish engulfing scenario. In Figure 12, the initiation of the bullish micro trend occurs with the first candle closing above the blue box, denoting the high of the last significant bearish candle.

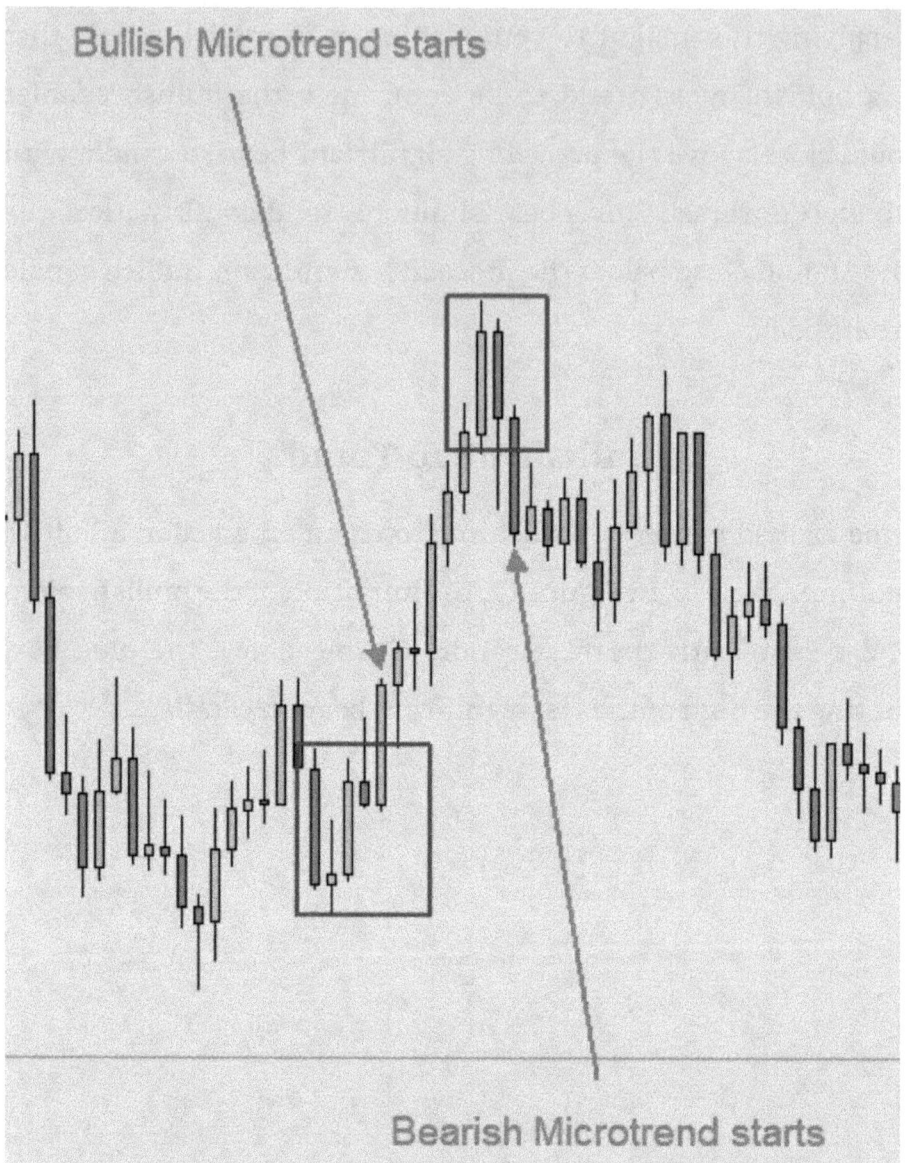

Figure 12: The beginning of a micro trend ends one price swing, and begins a new one.

Bearish Micro Trend

As highlighted previously, a bearish micro trend takes shape in a bearish engulfing scenario. In Figure 12, the onset of the bearish micro trend is marked by the first red candle closing below the blue box, representing the low of the last significant bullish candle.

When To Confirm A Bearish Micro Trend Change

A bearish micro trend change is validated when a bearish candle closes with its body below the low of a preceding major bullish candle. Refer to Figure 13.

In Figure 13, Candle B attempted but failed to close with its body below the last bullish candle, Candle A. However, Candle C successfully closed with its body below Candle A. This precise moment confirms the commencement of the bearish micro trend. Therefore, a bearish micro trend change is affirmed only if two conditions are met:

a. when the candle closes; and
b. the candle's body is below the low of last major bullish candle.

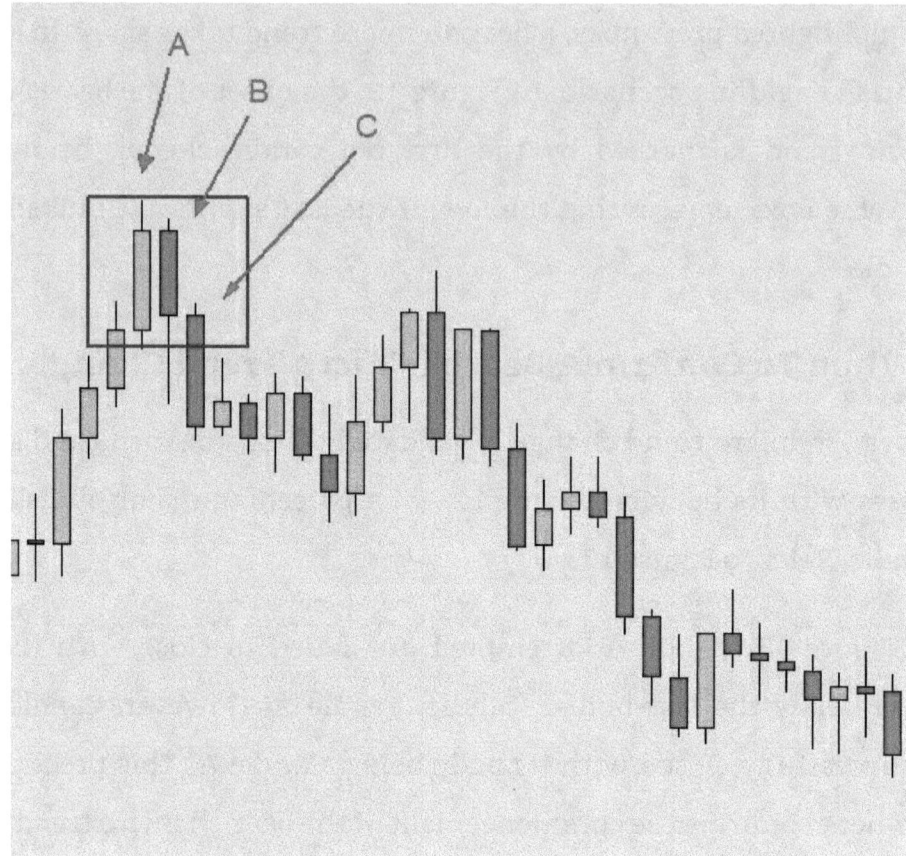

Figure 13: Candle C starting a bearish micro trend upon close

Watch the video titled *"Confirming a bearish micro trend change"* listed here, for a detailed demonstration of this concept.

When To Confirm A Bullish Micro Trend Change

A bullish micro trend change is substantiated when a bullish candle closes with its body above the high of a preceding major bearish candle. Refer to Figure 14.

In Figure 14, Candle C closed with its body above not only the last bearish candle, Candle B but also above Candle A. This precise moment confirms the termination of the bearish micro trend and the commencement of the bullish micro trend. Therefore, a bullish micro trend change occurs only if two conditions are met:

a. when the bullish candle closes; and

b. when the bullish candle's body is above the high of the last significant bearish candle.

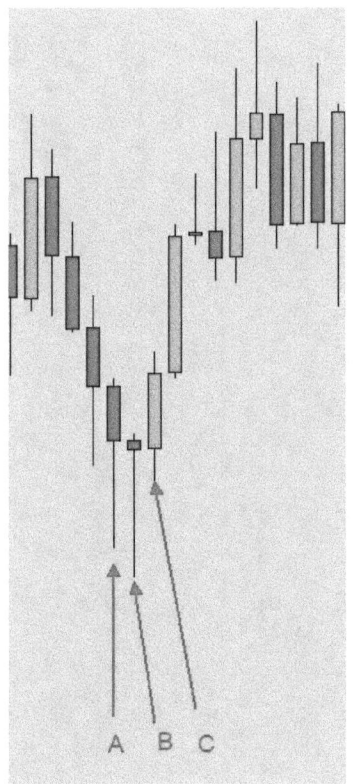

Figure 14: Candle C starting the bullish micro trend

Key Notes To Keep In Mind

This section is intentionally crafted to reinforce the crucial points discussed thus far. The central ideas I aim to underscore are:

a. The close of the candle.

b. The body of the candle closing above or below another candle or pivot point.

c. The last major (significant) candle.

a. The close of the candle

The close of a candle refers to the specific price at which a trading candlestick concludes its designated time period, whether it is a minute, an hour, a day, or another timeframe chosen by the trader. The candlestick consists of four main components: the open, close, high, and low prices during the given time interval.

"The close" specifically denotes the price level at the end of the chosen timeframe. If the close is higher than the open, the candlestick is typically coloured or represented as bullish (often green or white), indicating a price increase during that period. Conversely, if the close is lower than the open, the candlestick is usually coloured or represented as bearish (often red or black), suggesting a price decrease during that timeframe. Analysing the close of candles is fundamental to technical analysis in forex trading and is used to identify trends, potential reversals, and areas of support or resistance.

b. The body of the candle closing above or below another candle or pivot point.

Observing whether the body of a candle closes above or below another candle or a pivot point is essential for market analysis. If a candle's body closes above, it suggests potential upward momentum. Conversely, if it closes below, it indicates potential downward momentum. This information helps traders assess market direction and make informed decisions. Watch the video titled: *"The closing of the candle with its body"*, listed here, to understand this better.

c. The last major candle

The last major candle refers to the final significant candlestick in a given chart pattern or trend. Traders often pay close attention to this candle as it can offer crucial insights into potential trend reversals or the continuation of the existing trend. Analysing the patterns and closing behaviour of the last major candle provides valuable information for making informed trading decisions. Watch the video titled, *"The last major candle"*, listed here, to understand this better.

Knowing when the market direction shifts is imperative for making timely trading decisions. Emphasizing the three points above is absolutely paramount in achieving this understanding.

At the macro level, a substantial shift in trend becomes apparent when a candlestick closes above or below a preceding pivot point with its body. In an uptrend, if a candlestick closes below a previous pivot point with its body, the trend changes from an uptrend to a bearish trend. Conversely, in a downtrend, if a candlestick forms above a previous pivot point, the macro trend transitions from a downtrend to a bullish trend. It is crucial to zero in on the closing price in relation to the previous pivot point, specifically focusing on the candlestick's body, to ascertain the macro trend shift.

At the micro level, shifts in market direction are discerned through the analysis of engulfing patterns and the closing prices of candlesticks. In a bearish engulfing scenario, bearish candlesticks close below the low of the preceding bullish candlestick with their body, establishing the bearish micro trend. The bearish micro trend gains further confirmation when the price does not close above the previous candlestick with its body.

Conversely, in a bullish engulfing scenario, bullish candlesticks close above the previous bearish candlestick's high with their body, instituting the bullish micro trend. The bullish micro trend is further substantiated when the price tries but fails to close below the low of the last bullish candlestick with its body. These patterns signify the prevailing dominance of either bears or bulls at the micro level.

By recognizing these patterns and grasping the importance of candlestick closings with their bodies, traders can adeptly pinpoint changes in market direction at both macro and micro levels. This awareness facilitates timely adjustments to trading strategies and enables the seizing of potential opportunities in evolving market conditions.

Equipped with a comprehensive understanding of how to identify changes in market direction, let us progress to the next section, where we will delve into the concept of integrating micro and macro trends in trading.

CHAPTER FOUR

COMBINING MICRO AND MACRO TRENDS IN TRADING?

Integrating both micro and macro trends into your trading strategy can substantially elevate your likelihood of success. Although this material does not teach any specific trading strategy, its aim is to empower traders in precisely interpreting market structure. Let us briefly delve into how you can seamlessly fuse the macro trend with the micro trend in your trading approach.

To seamlessly integrate the macro trend with the micro trend, the first step is to determine the direction of the macro trend. This can be achieved by examining higher highs and higher lows or lower highs and lower lows on a higher timeframe. By now, you should be adept at identifying valid swings and pivot points, allowing you to pinpoint highs and lows in the market. This skill is crucial for comprehending price dynamics and laying a strong foundation for making well-informed trading decisions. As you advance in your forex journey, the ability to recognize these key elements will empower you to interpret market movements and trends with confidence.

Once the direction of the macro trend is identified, the subsequent step is to pinpoint the prevailing micro trend direction within that macro trend.

As highlighted earlier, the micro trend can be identified by scrutinizing engulfing patterns and candlestick formations on the same timeframe. By aligning the micro trend with the macro trend, traders can execute trades that harmonize with the overall market direction.

In my own trading methodology, I usually initiate trades on a smaller timeframe once I have established the directions of both the macro and micro trends on a higher timeframe. This approach enables me to identify optimal entry and exit points that align with current market conditions.

You can explore one of my most effective trading strategies here. As evident from the equity curve derived from over 20 years of back-testing, the profitability of this strategy speaks for itself, and I encourage you to give it a try.

By integrating both macro and micro trends into your trading analysis, you acquire a more comprehensive perspective of the market, enabling you to make informed trading decisions aligned with the prevailing market direction. For a practical demonstration of this concept, watch this video titled, *"Integrating both macro and micro trends into your trading"*, listed here, to understand this better.

Now that we have delved into the concept of combining micro and macro trends, let us proceed to the next section, where I unveil my naked exit strategy.

CHAPTER FIVE

THE NAKED EXIT METHOD

To exit trades objectively, it is crucial to flow with the market rather than relying on guesswork. Although the macro trend may be in an upward direction, it does not guarantee that the micro trend will automatically follow suit. In my trading approach, I close trades when the micro trend deviates from its course and no longer aligns with the direction of the macro trend. I avoid speculating that it will eventually revert and risk potential losses in the market.

When I am in a buy trade and the micro trend suddenly turns bearish, I execute my exit plan by closing the trade. Similarly, if I am in a sell trade and the micro trend unexpectedly turns bullish, I exit the trade immediately. This approach allows me to maintain a disciplined and objective stance, safeguarding my investment from unfavourable market movements.

I use this exit approach in my trading system introduced earlier.

By being responsive to changes in the micro trend and aligning my exit decisions with the macro trend, I aim to preserve capital and maximize trading opportunities. This proactive approach ensures that I exit trades promptly when market dynamics no longer support my initial trade thesis.

In my trading, I often go for a 1:2 risk-to-reward ratio, and I also trail my stops. However, whether I have my 1:2 risk-to-reward ratio in place or not, when I see a micro trend set up against the direction of my trade, I consider that a must-exit.

Watch the video titled *"Exiting trades objectively"* listed here, to learn about my exit method.

I would like to emphasize that this is not the sole objective method for exiting trades. Numerous alternatives exist. For instance, in one of my trading systems that involves the AUDJPY pair on the daily chart, I utilize an ATR (Average True Range) indicator. This involves adjusting my stops as the ATR indicator follows the candle movements. The key lies in identifying the objective approach that suits you best and applying it to your trading strategy.

Now that we have discussed the importance of objectively exiting trades, let us move on to the next section, where a valuable secret is revealed.

CHAPTER SIX

AN IMPORTANT TRADING SECRET

The information I am about to share holds the status of a closely guarded secret, as it is not readily available in the public domain. Discovered years after completing several trading courses, this insight eluded me during my trading education. To my astonishment, I stumbled upon it through years of hands-on experience, marking a pivotal moment six years into my trading journey. I am confident that unveiling this knowledge will substantially contribute to your trading success.

It is universally acknowledged that no trading system can guarantee a 100% success rate. Additionally, every trading strategy harbours the potential for significant profitability. I was amazed to find out in my trading journey that most of my most respected trading gurus had 45% win rate. Some also had 65% win rate. This underscores the notion that the ability to trade profitably with a system hinges on the instrument traded and the timeframe utilized. While your existing trading system may boast considerable profitability, it is crucial to address the challenge of consistently trading it profitably. I want to emphasize that, akin to any other trading system, your current trading approach holds the potential for extraordinary profitability. Each trading system can deliver substantial profits on specific pairs and timeframes but may not perform optimally on others.

In the pursuit of profitable trading, your initial objective should be to pinpoint the pair(s) or timeframes where your system exhibits profitability and concentrate exclusively on trading within those parameters. Rigorous back-testing of your trading system across various financial assets and timeframes is instrumental in identifying the ones that align most effectively with your strategy.

In essence, every highly profitable strategy is tailored to specific pairs and timeframes where it thrives. The performance of your current system whether struggling on certain pairs or excelling on others, does not inherently indicate its overall effectiveness. Similarly, discovering a highly profitable trading system on a specific timeframe does not guarantee success on different timeframes of the same pair or on other pairs. This revelation underscores a crucial secret: your mission is to uncover the pair(s) and/or timeframe(s) where your system excels.

To facilitate this exploration, I highly recommend Soft4fx Simulator, an exceptional tool in my experience. Offering a one-time payment for lifetime access, this simulator is invaluable for conducting thorough back-testing, allowing you to assess the effectiveness of your trading system across different pairs or financial assets. If you choose to make a purchase through my provided link, I may receive a small commission. Feel free to reach out with any questions, and I will be more than happy to assist you. The simulator's responsive support team is also readily available to address any queries or concerns, even during weekends.

By concentrating on the assets or pairs where your trading system exhibits profitability and conducting meticulous back-testing, you can refine your trading approach and enhance your chances of success. With this enlightening secret unveiled, let us move forward to the next section, where additional valuable insights will be shared to elevate your trading knowledge and success.

CHAPTER SEVEN

RISK MANAGEMENT &
TRADING PSYCHOLOGY

I n my years exploring the dynamic realm of trading, I have gained valuable insights into two crucial elements: understanding the psychology of trading and mastering the essential skill of risk management. I am thrilled to share straightforward insights that I genuinely believe will have a positive impact on your trading.

The key to successful trading lies in establishing clear rules and steadfastly adhering to them. Understanding your trading system's capabilities, including its tolerance for consecutive losses, empowers you to face losing trades with confidence, knowing that recovery is within reach. This knowledge constitutes a valuable secret that can profoundly influence your trading outcomes.

Furthermore, I want to re-emphasize the immense value of back-testing your trading strategy. This practice is a game-changer for your trading psychology as it acquaints you with your system, allowing you to trade without fear. Becoming comfortable with your own approach, is a crucial step toward confident and successful trading.

Moreover, it is crucial to establish a maximum percentage of your capital that you are willing to risk for each trade. By implementing effective risk management practices, you protect your capital and mitigate the impact of potential losses.

Integrating these risk management considerations into your trading rules and steadfastly adhering to them will significantly enhance your chances of success.

Remember, successful trading is not just about strategy and analysis; it also involves managing risk and maintaining a disciplined trading psychology. By combining sound risk management principles with a strong trading mind-set, you set yourself on a path towards consistent profitability.

In a nutshell, getting to know your trading system thoroughly and sticking to its rules is key. A good trading system should be rule-based. It should not allow room for guessing; either the setup is there, or it is not. This is why I firmly believe in the excellence of my trading system – it is the mechanical trading system I had always dreamed of having. Check it out here.

CHAPTER EIGHT

FINAL THOUGHTS & FAQS

Throughout this course, you have acquired valuable knowledge on reading market structure effectively. You have delved into market swings, pivot points, and the art of determining market direction at both macro and micro levels. Applying this knowledge to your trading strategy, you now understand the importance of initially identifying market structure at the macro level, followed by the micro level, and executing trades on a lower timeframe.

Another vital lesson learned is how to exit trades objectively, ensuring disciplined and systematic decision-making. The accompanying videos listed here, have been meticulously prepared to provide comprehensive explanations of each topic covered in this material, enhancing your understanding and learning experience. More videos and exercises and worksheets will be added to our YouTube channel and you can find more resources on the videos page to dress any gaps you may have about the principles shared in this guide.

By synthesizing these concepts and incorporating them into your trading approach, you have the potential to develop a powerful trading strategy. Remember, no trading system is infallible, but by honing your skills, conducting thorough analysis, and adhering to a well-defined plan, you can increase your chances of success.

Embarking on your trading journey armed with the knowledge acquired from this course is a significant step toward success. By understanding market structure, identifying pivotal points, and mastering the art of reading both macro and micro trends, you have equipped yourself with essential tools.

Remember, successful trading is a continuous journey of learning, adapting, and disciplined execution. May your trades be profitable, and your path in the dynamic world of trading be rewarding. Happy trading!

You can join our trading community, listed here, and ask any questions you might have about this course.

Frequently Asked Questions

Based on what you have learned so far, here are 10 frequently asked questions and answers to refresh your mind.

1. What is a valid pivot point?

Answer: A valid pivot point is a price level where the market reverses its direction, creating a noticeable gap between at least two candles within the swing. It indicates a significant shift in market momentum.

2. How can I determine the bigger direction of the market?

Answer: The market direction can be determined by observing whether the market is forming higher highs and higher lows (indicating a macro uptrend) or lower highs and lower lows (indicating a macro downtrend).

3. How do I know when the market direction changes?

Answer: At the macro level, a change in trend direction is observed when a candlestick closes above or below a previous pivot point with its body. At the micro level, changes in market direction can be identified through engulfing patterns and the closing prices of candlesticks.

4. How can I combine micro and macro trends in my trading?

Answer: To combine micro and macro trends, first identify the direction of the macro trend by analysing higher highs and higher lows or lower highs and lower lows. Then, determine the micro trend within that macro trend and execute trades that align with both trends.

5. How can I exit a trade objectively?

Answer: To exit trades objectively, flow with the market rather than relying on guesswork. Close a buy trade if the micro trend suddenly turns bearish and exit a sell trade if the micro trend unexpectedly turns bullish.

6. Can any trading system guarantee 100% accuracy?

Answer: No, no trading system can guarantee 100% accuracy. It is essential to identify the pair(s) or assets where your system demonstrates profitability and focus on trading those pairs.

7. How can I determine the profitability of my trading system on different pairs?

Answer: Thorough back-testing of your trading system on different pairs can help you identify the pairs on your system performs best. Consider using a reliable simulator, like Soft4fx Simulator, to conduct comprehensive back-testing.

8. Question: Why is it important to focus on the pairs and timeframes where my trading system demonstrates profitability?

Answer: Focusing on profitable pairs allows you to optimize your trading approach and increase your chances of success. Not all pairs may be suitable for your system, so identifying the profitable ones helps you focus your efforts.

9. Question: What are some key takeaways from this course?

Answer: Key takeaways include understanding valid pivot points, determining trend direction at both macro and micro levels, combining micro and macro trends, exiting trades objectively, and recognising that no trading system is infallible.

10. Question: What advice would you give to ensure my trading success?

Answer: Concentrate on discovering a rule-based trading system and commit to adhering to its rules.